BARRON'S
BOOK OF CARTOONS

PRENTICE HALL PRESS

Library of Congress Cataloging-in-Publication Data

Barron's book of cartoons / by the editors of Barron's.
    p. cm.
   ISBN 0-7352-0142-0 (cloth)
    1. Barron's (Chicopee, Mass.) 2. Business Caricatures and
cartoons. 3. Investments Caricatures and cartoons. 4. American
wit and humor, Pictorial. I. Barron's Educational Series, inc.
II. Barron's (Chicopee, Mass.) III. Title: Book of cartoons.
NC1428.B33B37 1998
741.5'973—dc21   99-37447
                                      CIP

Printed in the United States of America

10 9 8 7 6 5 4 3 2

ISBN 0-7352-0142-0   0-13-087204-0 (Barron's)

PRENTICE HALL PRESS
Paramus, NJ 07652

On the World Wide Web at http://www.phdirect.com

People who don't read *Barron's* might be surprised to find cartoons in such a highly respected business magazine, but they shouldn't be. Cartoonists and journalists alike benefit from seeing humor in the world around us. The same goes for readers.

A lot of what we see on Wall Street is nothing short of comical, and it's our job to point that out. Chief executives make promises they know they will never keep. Analysts gush about highly questionable stocks. Investors are sure the bull market will never stumble. Such bubbles beg to be burst, and, in *Barron's*, it is often a cartoonist's pen that does the pricking.

Barron's seeks to put the machinations of the business world into perspective, oftentimes making news in the process. It's no secret that stocks move on Monday mornings in reaction to *Barron's* stories that have appeared over the weekend. The magazine's profusion of profitable insights helps explain why the average reader spends two and a half hours poring over each issue. They don't read just for profit, though. They read for enjoyment, for entertainment, for knowledge. Many of them also read for the cartoons.

And why not? When high-flying technology stocks lose altitude, it helps to laugh about it, or at least commiserate with hundreds of thousands of fellow investors who are seeing the same cartoons.

The talented cartoonists who contribute their work to *Barron's* excel at capturing the thrill, the disappointment and, at times, the sheer lunacy of the business world. In this book, you will find some sterling examples, including Richard Cline's droll Wall Street barflies, who ruefully point out that you can't "buy at the bottom" unless you "have money at the bottom." Then there is Thomas Cheney's unruffled executive who calmly sits in an office surrounded by colleagues who are wildly throwing chairs and pointing fingers at one another. The fellow's wry comment: "As you may have already gathered, we're family-owned and -operated."

In a similar vein, Bernard Schoenbaum's aging tycoon says to the young man at his side, "Son, I had great plans for you, but I forgot what they were."

Not all cartoons in *Barron's* are about business. Whatever their subject, the best cartoons allow us to recognize ourselves, our loved ones, and our friends. A popular topic is relationships. Frank Cotham depicts a husband and a wife in a car that's been pulled over by a policeman. The husband's excuse to the officer: "I was driving under the influence of another person."

In another cartoon, Harley Schwadron's smiling husband generously tells his wife, "Honey, it's your birthday, cook anything you want for supper."

As with all humor, cartoons succeed when they strike an emotion inside us, be it overwhelming joy or deepest sorrow or something in between. Cartoons can help us better cope with a silly colleague, a pompous boss or a pointless business meeting. In poking fun at frustrating situations that have become so commonplace in the late 20th century, our cartoonists help readers to feel a sense of community, a sense of shared experience. And this remains central to *Barron's* mission of giving investors a front-row seat on Wall Street, the biggest show in business.

A common misconception is that *Barron's* has aisle after aisle of cartoonists laboring away in cubicles here at our headquarters in southern Manhattan.

The truth is that our cartoon contributors are spread all across the country, from Bethel, Connecticut, to Malibu, California. About midway between those two locales you will find Frank Cotham, who works out of a spare bedroom in his home in the Memphis suburb of Bartlett, Tennessee. Cotham, 50, started his career as a staff artist, creating graphics for a Memphis TV station. He would make cartoons in his spare time and submit them to magazines around the country. Cotham knew he was onto something in the late 1970s when, in a three-week stretch, he had cartoons accepted by the *Saturday Review*, the *Saturday Evening Post* and *Changing Times*. Today his work can be seen not only in *Barron's* but many other publications, ranging from *The New Yorker* to *The Bulletin of Atomic Scientists*.

In one sense, Cotham works around the clock. He carries a little spiral-bound notebook with him all day, and he keeps it on his bedstand at night so he can write down any nocturnal brainstorms. "The idea comes first," he explains in his courtly Southern voice. "Then I collect the scraps of paper, go through all the thoughts and start noodling with the most promising ones." Unlike some artists, Cotham keeps a highly regular schedule. He labors from about 8:30 in the morning until about 5:00 in the afternoon, and he takes an hour off to have lunch with his wife, who works about five minutes' drive from their home.

One guy who doesn't keep a regular schedule is Mike Shapiro, age 37, who works out of his apartment in Falls Church, Virginia, just nine miles from the White House. He often does cartooning late into the night for a number of weeks and then switches to more of a day shift. He draws his inspiration from newspapers, radio, and TV programs, and sometimes out of the blue. He will sit for three hours at a time with a white legal pad in front of him. "I have to wait until I get into that right mental state," he explains. "Sometimes I'll write 10 gag lines in two and a half hours, and all 10 will come in the last half hour."

Shapiro is always on the hunt for catchy phrases, ones that sound true to life but in reality are ridiculous. A good example is his cartoon in this book showing a straightlaced executive introducing a new man on the job to the company's director of operations. The caption reads, "This is Maurice. . . . He's a hugger."

The cartoonist with the most unusual sideline has to be Leo Cullum. When he's not drawing in his studio overlooking the sea in Malibu, California, he can be found piloting flights for TWA from Los Angeles to New York. Before going to work at TWA in 1968, Cullum flew jets for the Marines.

We recently caught up with him in St. Louis, where he was completing training to captain the airline's Boeing 767s.

Now 58, Cullum is always on the lookout for words that have entered our vocabulary in recent years, like "paradigm," for example. Cullum asks with a laugh, "What was it we used to say before we said 'whatever'?"

Cullum usually works in his home studio, accompanied by his yellow Labrador retriever, Winnie, and the strains of jazz or big-band music. The studio is in the basement, but because Cullum's house is built into a hillside, he can look out from his workspace and see the Pacific Ocean. "We're only about one mile inland, but it's very rural up here," he explains. "You see deer and bobcat, and occasionally rattlesnakes."

On the walls of Cullum's studio hang framed cartoons by other artists, including one by Edward Sorel and an original Charles Addams. "Charles gave me that in about 1972," Cullum recalls. "I didn't realize that it would become so valuable." The two men met a few years earlier, when Cullum first began cartooning for *The New Yorker*.

Cullum doesn't require the work of great cartoonists or the wild outdoors for inspiration. He has been known to dash off cartoons from a hotel room while he's on the road for TWA. "As long as there's a fax machine in the hotel, it's fine," he says.

Many readers ask us how we select cartoons here at *Barron's* . The process begins with Art Director Pamela Budz, who reviews the foot-high stack of submissions that arrives each week. She feels that the most successful cartoons lampoon some aspect of business, investing, or the broader human experience. She looks for a simple, direct connection between a cartoon's words and its art. When cartoons work, she says, they eloquently capture reality in "an undeniably funny way."

Pam's favorite cartoons land on my desk, but they don't stay there long. While I have been known to procrastinate over many a task, including writing this introduction, that's never been the case with cartoons. I always welcome "cartoon duty" as a respite from just about anything else I'm doing.

For me, there is no single litmus test that a cartoon must pass. Some make me laugh out loud. That's a good sign. Others produce a grin and make me think anew about a given topic, whether it be the cost of college tuition or how silly the job-interview process can be. Our final picks, about seven a week, are then made ready for publication.

So far, our selection process has produced good results. Readers often write to tell us how much they loved a particular cartoon. And it's not unusual to see a *Barron's* cartoon taped to an office door or to a refrigerator. We've heard that our cartoons frequently make it into business presentations, too.

With reader enthusiasm like this, you can understand why we wanted to publish this book. The idea came from Ellen Schneid Coleman of Prentice Hall. Our view was that *Barron's* cartoons have brought such pleasure to us and to our readers that we would be happy to have them reach a broader audience.

We dedicate this book to the cartoonists whose talents have made our lives a little brighter over the years, and we hope this collection makes your life a little brighter, too.

EDWIN A. FINN, JR.
EDITOR AND PRESIDENT, *BARRON'S*

"I believe Dijon is available at our Madison Avenue location."

"The stock market went down today, on fears that it would go down."

"Love is a rose – that's all we really know about it."

"These are artistic people. Use the word 'montage'."

"This is Morris, our director of operations. He's a hugger."

"Let's face it, Charles, nothing makes you 'reach for your wallet.'"

"As you may have already gathered, we're family-owned and -operated."

"Gotta go, Eddie. I like to be the first one in the office."

"Oh, I don't know, Tom. Living close to the edge isn't as bad as some would have you believe."

"It's your birthday? Cook anything you want for supper."

"Well, I guess I've taken up enough of your time."

"You remind me of myself at your age, Collins. You're fired."

"Must be one of those reverse commuters."

"I'm not jealous, I just didn't like the way you talked
about aggressive-growth bond funds with her."

"Your basic rule of thumb should be,
the bigger the guilt, the longer the stem."

"I'm planning to give birth right there at my desk."

"…and then one day I said to myself 'What is all this overwork and overachieving doing to me?' So I quit my job at the firm and here I am."

"*I think I speak for all bears when I say your use of our name to connote a lousy market is highly insensitive.*"

*In Grandma's day we survived without ever
sipping from a sports bottle."*

"You're the only one who doesn't hate me!"

"I broke through too many glass ceilings. And you?"

"Oh, Miss Saunders, when you say I'm away on vacation,
add 'well-deserved.'"

"Can you believe it? Since we installed our wood-burning stove
we've spent next to nothing on heating oil."

"Son, I had great plans for you, but I forgot what they were."

"What happened, Caswell? You were in charge of the feng shui."

"Sorry, Dr. Dudley doesn't treat original diseases.
He treats side effects from other doctors' treatments."

"Two pieces of carry-on. What's the problem?"

"Ignore him. He does that with every check."

"Judging by my allowance, Dad, you look like a man trapped
in a low-yielding financial portfolio."

*"Balancing work and family has become easier since
I lost my job and my wife left with the kids."*

"Sorry... right now, they're engaged in a power struggle."

"I was driving under the influence of another person."

"How about a burger before we get down to business?"

"What we have here is a quantity of life issue."

"I'm here, honey …in the media room."

"I used to drive a hearse – this is pretty much the same thing."

"You think it's easy, reeling in this enormous ego,
even for an evening with your friends?"

"Let's get married, I'm tired of being charming."

"We got a runaway..."

"*Choking, sir? I believe Raymond is your waiter.*"

"I'm sorry, Ma. I won't be able to do your taxes this year."

"Big money, sir ....Riggs and Patterson have picked up the scent!"

"Remarkable …a pacemaker/pager combo!"

"We feel advertising that insults the customers' intelligence distracts them from the high cost of the product."

"Yes, madam, Teletubbies."

"I don't mind you taking home what you don't eat.
What I mind is you taking home what everyone else doesn't eat!"

"Here's something else you should never do
with your eyeglasses."

"Got a minute, Ferguson?"

"Careful pal, you're talking about the stocks I love."

"I wouldn't say the stock is doing badly. I would just say
that it hasn't been embraced by the street."

"I'll tell you the meaning of life if you tell me
why you wear your cap backwards."

"I'll tell you something, I feel at home here already!"

"If I want feedback, Mansfield, I'll pay a consultant for it."

"In the interest of diversity, we try not to hire too many relatives."

"I knew it would be bad, but I definitely wasn't prepared
for software manuals."

"This looks good. It's a six-hour special on
how Americans are becoming too sedentary."

"Not much, just sitting around allowing myself to be manipulated by the media."

"Oh, for God's sake, Henry — do you think Alan Greenspan is lying awake nights worrying about what you're going to do?"

"You're very observant. Most people never notice
the color of my socks."

"You know what I'd love? I'd love a bowl of mineral water."

"By the end of the day it's hard to tell the fatigued
from the bored and the medicated."

"Hey, can I get back to you? I think the restructuring has begun."

"Sorry, Frank, I didn't mean that…it was the money talking."

"Oh, sure, he seems like fun now,
but how will he perform in a down market?"

"My name is Carl, and I'll be the guy you'll be trying to find all night."

"We're not looking for someone who wants to run with the wolves.
We're looking for someone who wants to run them over."

"Remember, you can fool some of the people all of the time.
Those are the people we need to concentrate on."

"Oh, that. Just the remnants of a rather messy
business meeting I had this morning."

"I've got a governor on line two, contemplating a property tax increase."

COURT T.V.

REGULAR · HI DEFINITION

"It was right here, when we received our first call from '60 Minutes'."

"Oh, look, Alan! There seems to be a large, exciting city right outside our window."

"I'd love to hear about the wife and kids, Mr. Todd,
but we've been instructed to can the chatter."

"*Tourists! For God's sake, put it out!!*"

"People in L.A. can fool you sometimes,
they seem very laid back but they're really dead."

"It happened either over the weekend
or when I left the office today for lunch."

"Here's a little bit of the glue that holds everything together."

"Of course, we'd make better time if we weren't towing the press barge."

"You have to have money at the bottom if you want to buy at the bottom."

"Actually I don't smoke. I just like to goof off in front of the building."

"Our stock has jumped six points on the rumor that you've resigned."

"No, sweetheart, it's a game about real estate, not Microsoft."

"*The boys from Burbank are here to see you.*"

"You know what golf needs? Fights."

"Some things, Morris, are more easily expressed through puppets."

"Okay. Heads, we take a tiny pay cut, tails, we
fire most of the work-force."

"When Paulson comes in let's all pretend to be speaking French."

"How do you do, sir? My name is John L. Flagman,
and I run a successful executive search firm."

"I'm taking my Viagra with Prozac. If it doesn't work, I don't care."

List of Illustrators

BUSINESS REPLY MAIL
FIRST CLASS MAIL PERMIT NO. 26 CHICOPEE MA

POSTAGE WILL BE PAID BY ADDRESSEE

BARRON'S
ATTN: SUBSCRIBER SERVICES
P.O. BOX 7014
CHICOPEE, MA 01021-9901